When the Jonquils Bloomed

Samantha Wilson

Presentation by *BookLeaf Publishing*

Web: www.bookleafpub.com

E-mail: info@bookleafpub.com

ISBN: 9789358367300

First edition 2023

For my Mama.

The D Word

I did the dishes
I opened the blinds
and let in the sunshine
Had it been so dark this whole time
My hands shook with each stroke of the sponge
against the few ceramics which had
somehow survived my clumsy hands
And finally he sat with me
as I'd begged him before.
But no amount of time now
could mend the brokenness
My mind wandered
as my tears mixed with the soapy water
to the bowls that had slipped away
before I could catch them
I was never good at catching things
The coffee cups had chipped and
eventually I had to tearfully
toss them in the trash because they offered me
less coffee and more mess
Each dish that had survived though
their strength in their greyness
and plainness
surviving me, of all things

"I just want to do the dishes"
I thought it came out as a scream
because that's what I was feeling
as he stifled me with his apologies
But it was a whisper
A faded distant voice
from fallen happy memories
Rotten apples from a dying tree

And we made plans for the future
together but separately
Two chipped coffee mugs
Offering more mess
and less coffee

Waving Through The Window

I have watched this scene play out a thousand times
And I am always
inside looking out
through the window to the back porch
And there we sit
Just you and me
And in this scene
we never touch
Just smile and throw our heads back laughing
A toast of bourbon
and cigar smoke dancing
I see myself tuck my frizzled hair behind my ear
And catch a glimpse of
happiness
in the innocence
of freedom and permission
to take up space
to speak
to just exist

But if we were to touch
I'd imagine it would be gentle
A soft hand wandering mindlessly

to connect each other
and conversation continuing
If I were to guess
Sometime in the night
the firepit we'd been watching flicker
would die down so tenderly
Embers shining through our empty bourbon glasses
Your exquisite bourbon glasses
And for a moment
we'd stay there
Lacing our fingers
and breathing

If I were to imagine just one more minute of this scene
I'd see myself tuck my head to your shoulder
and you'd graze my chin so slightly
And the embers burning would reflect in your sometimes hazel
sometimes brown eyes
And I'd close mine
And you'd kiss me

Making me long for the taste again
of cigars and whiskey
But this time so differently
This time is you and me
and it doesn't hurt

and it's soft and sweet

I've watched it play out a thousand times
Never letting us touch
But if we did
I'd light up like the cigar
and dance around like smoke
to feel the softness of your touch
And I wouldn't have to wonder
how the bourbon tastes
from your lips
And I could sit next to you finally
outside looking in

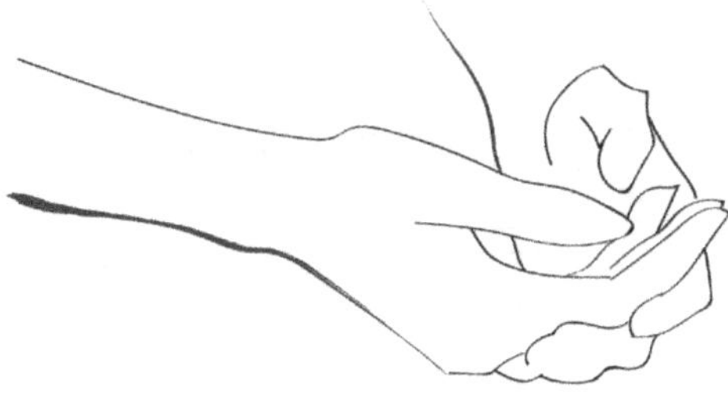

One Moment

There was a moment this morning
when my head was on her chest
and she held me tightly
that I realised there were no thoughts in my head
It only was her heartbeat
and her breath
My brain has never been
at peace
There is always something to do
An appointment to make
A dark cloud casting over happy thoughts
But this moment
was peace in the chaos

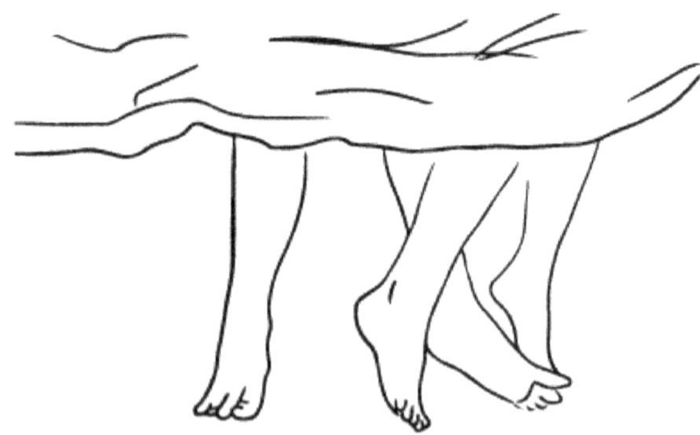

Apples and Oranges

I hate to compare
But there are some things
That are like switches
Dark and light
He told me to slow down
Rest
Take breaks
She told me
Keep going
You're on fire
Live your life

He snuffed out sparks
She lit the fires

He didn't see me
I'm all she sees

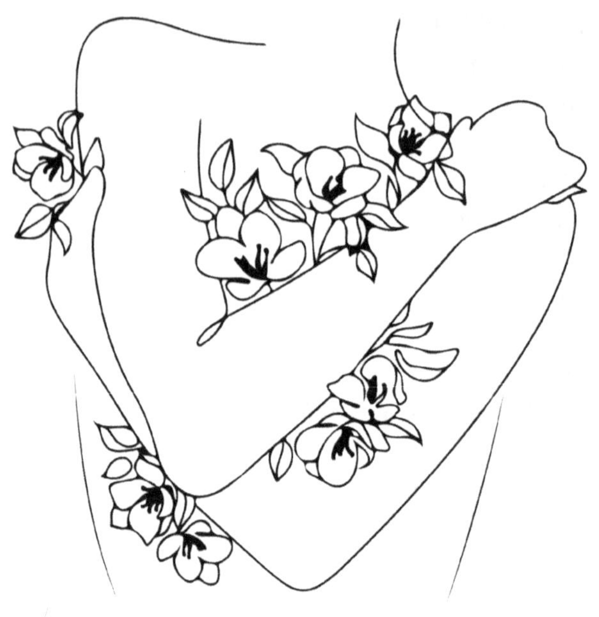

Torrential Downpour

Purple couch
Breathe
This is the first time I've been alone
I cannot cry
Do I feel...peace
For a moment I felt her
touch my leg
And I felt the warmth from her hand
Not her hand
Maybe God's
Ha. God. He didn't do this

I keep listening to Hamilton
It does and it doesn't makes sense
"He got better but his mother went quick"
But not my mother
She didn't go quickly
She let water fill her lungs
Seat belted in her blue car
Not the red one
Because the red one was not hers
I bet she wore my shoes
How selfish
To ruin such good shoes
That I could've used

How selfish

I keep having a thought
and it keeps leaving
Like her
Leaving me
In this mess
In this torrential downpour
Is this what she felt
The weight of the rain
and no other way to escape

Why didn't she speak to me
Because I have been called sunshine
And all she saw was rain

There are all these people
Telling me they are sorry
and that is for them
They don't know what to say
and I keep having to tell them
"It's okay."
Because they want to know they have
successfully prayed away
This emptiness
That my mother isn't dead
and I am suddenly
okay
This isn’t the tomb

on Easter Sunday
I don't have an umbrella
I didn't pray for this rain
I didn't know
crops needed watering
Because she would never say
A week ago, I was angry
As she was slipping away
When will this anger go away
When will I break
and cry
and feel the weight
When it does
Will it be a torrential rain

February 7

This isn't real
But here you are
Driving me places
To the funeral home
To get coffee
To make sure I've eaten
To make sure I sleep
To kiss me and make me forget that for one
damn moment
this isn't the reality
You took me to slam coffee mugs on the ground
and like it was nothing, you picked up the
broken glass
like picking up my own broken pieces
and placed them gently in a box in your trunk
You're not afraid of getting cut

As you left today and I caught a glimpse of the
carried weight
My carried weight
Your eyes were weary from the days' events
There was no lung capacity
just a hollow cavity when my insecurities
overwhelmed me momentarily
And I just knew you would tell me

That you couldn't handle this much
...messy

But here you are
A good morning message
Planned coffee
A moment of intentionality to ourselves
Ourselves
M.B. and me.

Leftovers

I put groceries away
and was overwhelmed with the thoughts
of people caring for me
so deeply
They sent me eggs
and what a funny thing to think
But it's 2023
I've done nothing to deserve
overflowing kindness
Except that my mother has died
But now my sister is here
and her children
and I hadn't thought of how I'd feed them
and then food just arrived

I cleaned the area around the coffee maker
Because that's the most important area
Where we gather
Where we brew more cups
Where the creamer at times has been
the only calories consumed

And like a regular night
I took a handful of vitamins
And I tucked children into bed

But it's not a regular night
There will never be another regular night again

I am weary of finding a new normal
I am weary of fighting for people to stay alive
There is a reason I'm good at psych
This. This is why.
The crisis that continue
Because the world doesn't stop
For a broken heart

And soon the overwhelming flood of love
will dissipate and I will be left
with moldy leftovers
and empty thank you notes to write
I'll be left to navigate without her
When she was so intrinsically my entire life

My aunt used to say
I called my mum too much
But I guess all the love
Every phone call
Was not quite enough

The Navy Dress

Yesterday we rewrote little moments
so that people in our pasts couldn't hold them anymore
I wore the floral navy dress
and fixed my hair
The floral navy dress should've gotten more recognition
the first time it was worn
and now it's sewn with threads of your whiskey breath
and soft hands
You wrapped your arms around my waist
and made me feel sexy
I wasn't sure we'd make it out of your bedroom

As I stood in your bathroom
I heard laughter and comfort
My best friend has never trusted others in such a way
and she rarely shares her real laugh
That's the comfort your home has brought
this weird collective of us
We all needed each other
And I deeply needed you

A Pandemic

We shared kisses in your office
We stood beside each other and talked
about mental health with our friends
Just close enough for me to place
my hand in your pocket, as if it were mine
We passed my coffee cup across us
and took sips as we glanced at each other
Because in this room we couldn't share a kiss
but we could share a sip

You worried about me traveling alone
and our locations were shared
Officially official, you said and smiled

I spent the day staring at our friend and her
beautiful baby girl
And listened to your favourite songs as I drove
home

The group chat started building in number
And it became apparent
That there was something else we'd shared
Three years of negative tests
And today
in our February of madness
Two quick positive tests

Paternity Test

The irony of sending my mother flowers
For her funeral
When you left her at a port
With a baby in California
And made her further untrusting of men
And love
And gave her me
Her beacon. Her hope
You never sent her flowers
For her to breathe and smell
And know she was loved
But today
As her ashes sit in my passenger seat
The flowers you sent her
Are next to me

Run On Sentences

And I have her military flag
And I have all these flowers that need to be
kept alive
I'm not good at keeping things alive
And I have too many throw away dishes now
And the calls have stopped
like I knew they would
And here I am
COVID positive
Sick baby girl
Restless baby boy
Alone in this house
with ashes and flowers

The Jonquils Bloomed

Someone, all of them, they all keep saying
How are you
and I reply flatly
The damn jonquils bloomed
They look at me with confusion
And pat my arm, and reach for my hand
And leave everything they are thinking left
unsaid

The thing about jonquils
They get mowed down
Ours specifically so close to the ground
I was certain they wouldn't possibly rise this
year
Resilient they are, though
And I saw the greens start to show
February is a tad early, I thought
But then again, what do I know

I said
This year
I wasn't going to be resilient
I was tired of surviving
I was ready for thriving
This year

I will throw my head back laughing
Let the wind
Tangle my blonde waves
Feel again sunshine on my face
This year, I wrote in a journal,
I will just be

February is a little early
For a mother to stop replying
For the analogy of drowning
to be something worth rewriting
And of course
Like every year
The damn yellow flowers
Appeared
The ones she would pick
and keep fresh
through all of spring
Isn't it a funny thing
How long she was resilient
How many years she continued to come back
Like the greens
and the flowers
And one day
the world stopped for her
But the world kept in motion for me
And all around me
There were flowers
down a path

And my daughter picks them and she laughs
and she has no idea
how lonely they make me
Because are filled with
the resilience
she couldn't keep facing

The thing about jonquils
They continue to bloom
And I am in a world of yellow flowers
Where there is no more you

Back Porch

Take out
on the back porch
I don't know if you caught my smile
as the wind grazed us
For a brief second
it wasn't too cold on a winter night
I've dreamt of moments
Of this moment
Of sitting across from you
on your back porch
It's one of your favourite places
and I wanted to be the one
with you sharing space
In this moment
I told you
I'd live life again
if it meant I ended up with you
and you know I don't say things I don't mean
and I smiled tonight
under the stars
as the geese flew above us
and thought
I can't wait for you
To one day marry me

Five Year Plans

I've barely slept
The clothes keep piling up
Because the kids are sick
My lungs felt heavy today
And I screamed at the toddler babe for fighting me
over putting his diaper back on
You texted me
Go to my house
Take the laundry
I'll do it for you
and you'll rest
And that seems so simple to you
It made sense
But my brain couldn't make sense today
And tears slipped from my eyes
over my weary face
and how the tears they burned my eyes
because I'm sleep deprived
And when I entered your home
My home
Because it is you and you are home
We hugged
The tension fell away
along with the thoughts of the day

It was the first moment I'd had
of full clarity today

You kissed me
as your red towel struggled around me
to hide my just showered body
You held me as I slept
peacefully and without vigilance
You kissed me
slowly awake
I want all of these moments
all of these days
the ease of breathing in
while in your embrace

To hell with your five year plan
Let's plan together
Let's make good on promises
And I'll kiss you when you come home
And you'll hug my kids, our kids
I'll have a beer opened
and you'll start the grill

Every version of my daydreamed future
Is filled with you in it
And I'm not good at planning
But baby, I'll make a plan if you're in it

First Christmas Gifts

I ordered a knife set
and I laughed
and I cried
Because a knife set was the first
Christmas gift
To my mom from my dad

Someone explain how we went from
knife sets
Practical loving gifts
Fishing days
And sun kissed faces

To a mother's suicide
To a dad getting high
on the way to his own grave

Forgetting that we needed him to kiss our boo
boos
When we fell from our bikes
We needed him to steady us
When our shoes were untied
I needed them in every audience
No matter how small my part
And we need him to hold us now

When I'm desperately trying to
hold together my heart

When I came home he told me
You're in your safe place now
And he has ripped away the safety nets

How did we go from love
and Christmas gifts
to this
Emptiness

Little Rock

This is one of your favourite places
The Little Rock tour
With you
Bourbon didn't taste right
and I thought you'd cry
But it's something we share
Like the only think I like about you
is your impeccable taste for expensive bourbon
We also share
A bed
A pillow
Water bottles
Breaths
Laughter
Moments. And I want all of them
We talked about childhood things
in comfy chairs
in the rooftop bar
and overlooked the city
You love the city
I love the way city lights reflect off your eyes
I love the smiles you make
and the confidence you have when you order
And the waitress treats us extra kind
Because we both stare at her and smile

Together or separate?
Oh, we are definitely together

Like Home and Earl Grey Tea

I called in with sickness
and although you aren't the cure
you ease my aching bones
And kiss my forehead gently
And make me earl grey tea
You've been planting earl grey tea
as a trigger of you for my memory
And I joke that you cannot break up with me
because I'm not giving up earl grey tea
But also
Please don't ever break up with me
I am 30 and once again thinking these things
like a lovestruck teen
Starting over with you
is one of the few things
that I'm sure of
And if you asked me a year ago
I would've said I never want to lose this friend
Ask me a year ago
If I'd believe in falling in love again
and my answer was
That isn't practical
That's a fairy tale dream

But here you are
so practically loving me
Waking up every day thinking
this has to be a dream
And here I am
eating my words
Capable again of falling in love
With the girl who feels like home
And tastes like earl grey tea

Grounding Techniques

Five shifts this week
Too many days without sleep
leading up to days that should be
Celebrations
Her birthday
Their anniversary
But she's gone
And there's little to celebrate

A planned 24 hours
To distract
To forget
To create new connections
with your family
To fill the gaps of my family

The weekend filled with normalcy
Dinner
Flirting over drinks
Kisses in between
Learning softball rules

It was the nightmare that jolted me
and reminded me
That normalcy is blanketing

Fear
Loss
Insecurity
That you'll leave me
I keep losing things
Insecurity
That I will lose you
And what's left of my heart
will like her, be gone too

You grounded me
You're good at grounding me
An anchor to reality
"I have you"
You whisper
And I know it to be true
And you walk me through my five senses
My heart and breathing ease
To normal rhythm
And your arms hold onto me
Until sunshine breaks through

She's More

You are my world, she said
I replied, you are my moon
and she put a question mark
next to the moon
Because she expected me to say
"You are my world, too"
But the thing about her

She's more than a world

My Moon

The moon
and the Earth
A delicate
and consistent love
For the entirety of their existence
The Earth
on an axis tilted
steadily turning and always
moving one day at a time
Despite destruction and decay
and changes along the way
And the moon
holding a firm grip on the gravity
of the axis
But never keeping the Earth from moving
Some would say the sun
is the reminder of hope
for new days to come
But really it is the moon
who allows rest and healing
And sees the darkest bits of earth
The moon is a lighthouse, a beacon
A reminder that stars are burning
and wishes can be made
The moon

She creates stability
She has seen the heartaches
Much closer than the sun could ever peek
And she pulls at the tides

In

and

Out

Reminding Earth to breathe

Triggers

There will always be water
There will always be thoughts
of how she could swim
The water was where she felt comfort
and free
And I could see the harsh lines on her face ease

There will always be water
Oceans
Lakes
Rivers

Rivers
Where the water moves swiftly
And instead of being swept away
She grounded herself
And I think of these things
Because she wouldn't have been swept away
She would have swam
Well damn
But a river
and a thought
combined
Oh how the water would wash away
Pain

Guilt
Wash away time
Years of wrongdoing
throughout her life
The water
Biblically
is what cleanses the sins
Before you enter you are marked with the world
And once you go under and come back again

Baptism
Freedom of chains that once held captive

And the thoughts
Combined
With the calm of the water
She set herself free

There will always be water
Taunting me and reminding me
Trying to trigger me
There will always be thoughts
Of what could be

www.ingramcontent.com/pod-product-compliance
Lightning Source LLC
LaVergne TN
LVHW011710230826
846092LV00010BA/1227

* 9 7 8 9 3 5 8 3 6 7 3 0 0 *